The Wondering Jew

Presents...

Ultimate

Torah Trainer

Bar/Bat Mitzvah Survival Guides

Elliott Michaelson

MAJS

THE ULTIMATE TORAH TRAINER

Copyright Information

MY PROGRESS

Date					
Torah blessings					
Torah reading					
Torah review in English					
Haftarah blessings					
Haftarah reading					
Haftarah review in English					

Date				
Torah blessings				
Torah reading				
Torah review in English				
Haftarah blessings				
Haftarah reading				
Haftarah review in English				

TERRIBLY CONVENIENT SOUND AND LETTER CHART

ה	ד	ג	בּ	בּ	א
H	D	G	V	B	...

	י	ט	ח	ז	ו
	Y	T	H̲	Z	V

ם	מ	ל	ך	כ	כּ
M	M	L	H̲	H̲	K

		ע	ס	ן	נ
		...	S	N	N

ץ	צ	ף	פ	פּ	
TZ	TZ	F	F	P	

ת	שׂ	שׁ	ר	ק	
T	S	SH	R	K	

TRANSLITERATIONS OF HEBREW VOWEL SOUNDS

(A very handy reference guide...)

E

Same sound as:
**SPECIAL
THEM
HEAD**

* Note that the *Shva* can also indicate the absence of a vowel sound.

O

Same sound as:
**HOPE
GROW
BOAT**

A

Same sound as:
**CUP
TROUBLE
SUPPER**

U

Same sound as:
**NOODLES
GROUP
SUPER**

I

Same sound as:
**MEATBALL
PIECE
AGREE**

AY

Same sound as:
**THEY
AGENT
STEAK**

* Some pronounce the *Tzayreh* as "E", some pronounce it as "AY", and some use both pronunciations.

AI

Same sound as:
**EYEBALL
RIGHT
LIBRARY**

Our *Bar/Bat Mitzvah Survival Guides* use the proper Hebrew names for people and places. The transliterations on this page will help you pronounce them properly. Sometimes, the English and Hebrew names are very close, but often they're quite different. Here are some of the most common differences.

Ashur	Assyria
Bavel	Babylon
Mitzra'im	Egypt
Moshe	Moses
Rivkah	Rebekah
Sha'ul	Saul
Shlomo	Solomon
Ya'akov	Jacob
Yehezk'el	Ezekiel
Yehoshu'a	Joshua
Yehudah	Judah
Yerushalayim	Jerusalem
Yirmiyahu	Jeremiah
Yish'ayah	Isaiah
Yisra'el	Israel
Yitzhak	Isaac
Yosef	Joseph

PUTTING ON THE TALLIT & TEFILLIN

If you've never had the chance to put on the *tallit* or *tefillin*, this is your lucky day! Traditionally, the *tallit* and *tefillin* are worn for all weekday morning services. On Shabbat and Holy Day mornings, only the *tallit* is worn (except Yom Kippur, when we wear the tallit all day). Why the difference? There are many explanations. My favorite reason goes like this: the Torah teaches us to wear reminders of our Divine Agreement with God on our arms and our heads (i.e. *tefillin*.) But on Shabbat, Pesah, Shavu'ot, Sukkot, Rosh Hodesh, Rosh Hashanah, and Yom Kippur, we perform rituals all day long that remind us of God's Agreement with us — so we don't need the *tefillin* to remind us. To put everything on, follow these basic steps. You can also find a video on our website at **http://www.adventurejudaism.net/Bar_Bat_Mitzvah_Guides.html**.

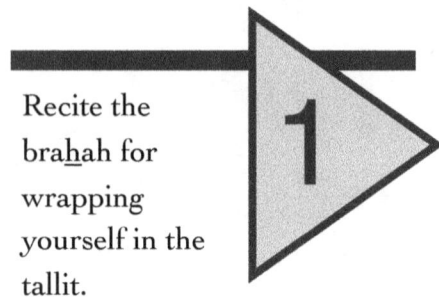

1

Recite the brahah for wrapping yourself in the tallit.

בָּרוּךְ אַתָּה יְיָ אֱלֹהֵינוּ מֶלֶךְ הָעוֹלָם, אֲשֶׁר קִדְּשָׁנוּ בְּמִצְוֹתָיו, וְצִוָּנוּ לְהִתְעַטֵּף בַּצִּיצִת.

We praise You, Adonai our God, Ruler of the universe, whose *mitzvot* make us holy, and who commanded us to cover ourselves with *tzitzit*.

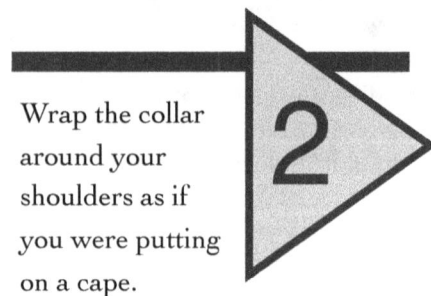

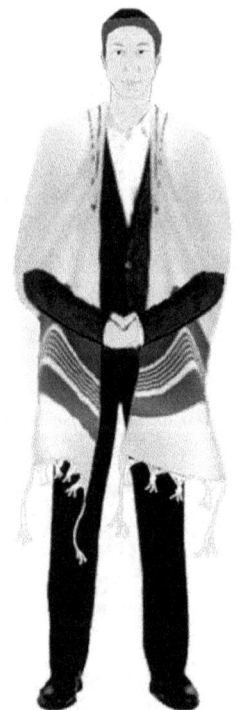

2

Wrap the collar around your shoulders as if you were putting on a cape.

On Shabbat and Holy Day mornings, stop here!

3

Loop the *tefillin shel yad* (the one with the extra-long strap) around your bicep.

If you're left-handed, use your right bicep. If you're right-handed, use your left bicep. If you're ambidextrous like me, take your pick!

4

Before tightening the loop, recite this bra<u>h</u>ah.

בָּרוּךְ אַתָּה יְיָ אֱלֹהֵינוּ מֶלֶךְ הָעוֹלָם, אֲשֶׁר קִדְּשָׁנוּ בְּמִצְוֹתָיו, וְצִוָּנוּ לְהָנִיחַ תְּפִלִּין.

We praise You, Adonai our God, Ruler of the universe, whose *mitzvot* make us holy, and who commanded us to put on *tefillin*.

5

Tighten the loop around your bicep and wrap the strap around your forearm 7 times.

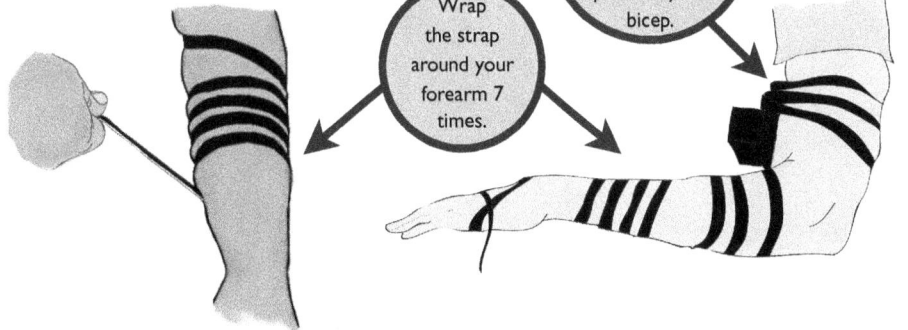

If the strap is long enough, use the extra length to keep the *tefillin* box in place on your bicep.

Wrap the strap around your forearm 7 times.

6

Place the *tefillin shel rosh* at the center of your forehead, right at the hairline.

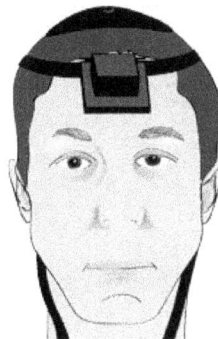

Two long straps extend from the back of the *tefillin shel rosh*. Let them hang freely on either side of your head.

7

Recite the brahah for the *tefillin shel rosh*.

בָּרוּךְ אַתָּה יְיָ אֱלֹהֵינוּ מֶלֶךְ הָעוֹלָם, אֲשֶׁר קִדְּשָׁנוּ בְּמִצְוֹתָיו, וְצִוָּנוּ עַל מִצְוַת תְּפִלִּין.

We praise You, Adonai our God, Ruler of the universe, whose *mitzvot* make us holy, and who commanded the *mitzvah* of tefillin.

8

Finish wrapping the *tefillin shel yad* by winding it around your middle finger 3 times.

If the strap is long enough, you can also wind it around your hand to help keep everything in place.

Tefillin shel rosh with the two hanging straps.

Tefillin shel yad around the bicep (under the tallit.)

Tefillin shel yad wrapped 3 times around the middle finger.

Tefillin shel yad wrapped 7 times around the forearm.

You're ready to go! When you're finished, take everything off in the reverse order.

D'VAR TORAH WRITING GUIDE

This guide is intended to give you a general idea of what a typical D'var Torah looks like. Yours may not look exactly like this — it will, of course, be written by you and not me! — but it should include all of these elements. As always, make sure you consult with your rabbi / teacher.

1. Don't thank people for coming — that's something you can tell your guests at the party afterwards. The person giving the D'var Torah is called a *Darshan* — literally, an "explainer". The congregation will thank *you* for explaining the weekly readings to *them*.

2. In one or two paragraphs, summarize the content of the Torah and Haftarah readings for that day.

3. Quote a verse or idea from the Torah and/or Haftarah in Hebrew and in English, and discuss its relevance in our times. This is when you bring in your own commentaries and tell us what you've learned from our ancient and modern teachers.

4. Explain how the idea you've chosen has meaning to you. You can discuss the impact the D'var Torah may have had on how you're going to lead your life, how it's affected your commitment to Judaism and its values, etc.

5. If it fits with your ideas, you may want to talk about your parents, grandparents or other family members and role models and what positive values or lessons you've learned from them. Note: this is not the same as thanking them. Save the "thank you's" for after the service!

6. Final thoughts: what does becoming a Bar/Bat Mitzvah mean to you? Why is it special to you and what have you learned in the process of studying for today? Typically, this is where you bring your discussion back to the original idea you chose from the Torah / Haftarah.

7. Your D'var Torah should be no more than four or five double-spaced pages — roughly the length of a five to seven minute speech.

My *parashah*, book from the Torah, and chapter/verse	
My *Haftarah* book and chapter/verse reference...	

What the TORAH says in my own words:

What the HAFTARAH says in my own words:

Questions I have about my TORAH reading, Haftarah, Bar/Bat Mitzvah process, or Judaism in general (minimum 3):	Questions my parents have about my TORAH reading, Haftarah, Bar/Bat Mitzvah process, or Judaism in general (minimum 3):

SECTIONS OF TORAH THAT STAND OUT FOR ME…

Chapter : Verse OR Section	What it says in my own words	Why it stands out for me

SECTIONS OF HAFTARAH THAT STAND OUT FOR ME…

Chapter : Verse OR Section	What it says in my own words	Why it stands out for me
↑	↑	↑
↑	↑	↑
↑	↑	↑

One idea or theme I want to talk about (based on my choices from charts 3 and 4):	
Verse or section from the Torah or Haftarah that relates to my theme (choose 1 or 2 from charts 3 and/or 4 and write them here):	

Commentator	The commentator's own words	What I think the commentator is trying to teach

One idea or theme I want to talk about: (copy from previous chart)	Verse or section from the Torah or Haftarah that relates to my theme: (copy from previous chart)

Commentator (copy from previous chart)	What I think the commentator is trying to teach (copy from previous chart)	How this teaching relates to my life or the world around me
↑	↑	
↑	↑	
↑	↑	

One idea or theme I want to talk about:
(copy from previous chart)

Verse or section from the Torah or Haftarah that relates to my theme:
(copy from previous chart)

Commentator (copy from previous chart)	**How this teaching relates to my life or the world around me** (copy from previous chart)

My lesson for this *parashah* (bring all your ideas together)

TA'AMEI HA-MIKRA: TROP CHARTS
TORAH TROP

Let's face it: learning trop can be very difficult. Most of us are used to the idea that each musical sign represents a single tone, but with trop, most signs (*ta'amim*) represent musical phrases. To add to the difficulty, there are 28 separate trop signs — each with a unique musical phrase, and sometimes the phrasing changes depending on the combination of *ta'amim* (though very few readings contain all 28 *ta'amim*). Sure, you can find sheet music to help you out, but if you're like me and don't read music, you might wind up more confused. Oy!

I developed the charts in this section to help people like me. Most of the *ta'amim* are grouped into sequences that are used commonly in the Tana<u>h</u>. The grids enable the teacher and the student to chart the music as it goes higher or lower.

These charts have proven quite helpful with my own students. I hope you find them just as useful!

אֶתְנַחְתָּא

Etna<u>h</u>ta divides a verse into two broad ideas. Tip<u>h</u>a, Zakef, Segol, and Shalshelet then divide Etna<u>h</u>ta into smaller ideas. Etna<u>h</u>ta always comes after Tip<u>h</u>ah.

Common Patterns
מֵירְכָא טִפְחָא מוּנַח אֶתְנַחְתָּא
טִפְחָא מוּנַח אֶתְנַחְתָּא
מֵירְכָא טִפְחָא אֶתְנַחְתָּא
טִפְחָא אֶתְנַחְתָּא
מוּנַח מוּנַח אֶתְנַחְתָּא

What's the point of all this trop?

Apart from musical notations, the trop (or, more properly, *te'amim*) tell us where to put the correct emphasis in each word and sentence. They also function as grammatical and syntactical notations, telling us when to pause in our reading, when to read quickly, etc. So we don't just read the punctuation — we sing it! There are seven distinct vocal systems for chanting the Tana<u>h</u>. Most people are familiar with Torah and Haftarah. See if you can find out what the other five are!

TORAH TROP

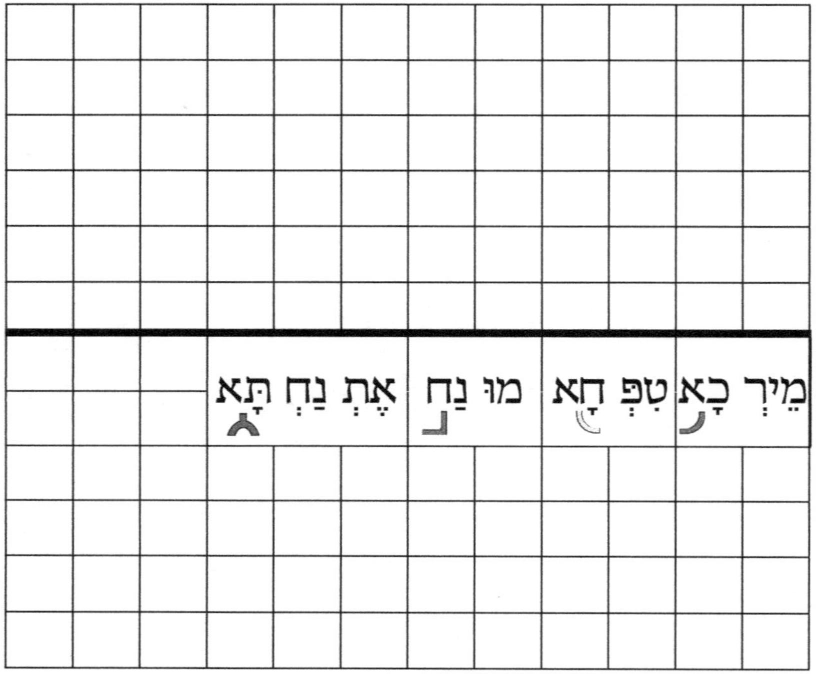

אֶתְנַחְתָּ֑א

Etnahta divides a verse into two broad ideas. Tipha, Zakef, Segol, and Shalshelet then divide Etnahta into smaller ideas. Etnahta always comes after Tiphah.

Common Patterns

מֵירְכָ֥א טִפְחָ֖א מוּנַ֣ח אֶתְנַחְתָּ֑א

טִפְחָ֖א מוּנַ֣ח אֶתְנַחְתָּ֑א

מֵירְכָ֥א טִפְחָ֖א אֶתְנַחְתָּ֑א

טִפְחָ֖א אֶתְנַחְתָּ֑א

מוּנַ֣ח מוּנַ֣ח אֶתְנַחְתָּ֑א

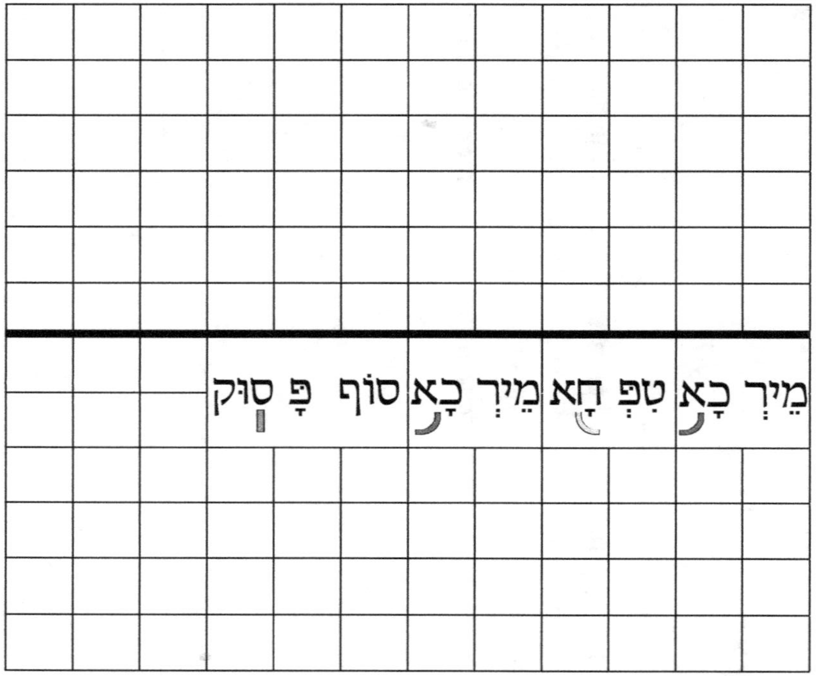

סוֹף-פָּסֽוּק

Sof Pasuk is also called סִילּוּק (Siluk). It marks the end of a verse. Tipha and Zakef subdivide Sof Pasuk into smaller ideas. Sof Pasuk always comes after Tiphah.

Common Patterns

מֵירְכָ֥א טִפְחָ֖א

מֵירְכָ֥א סוֹף-פָּסֽוּק

טִפְחָ֖א מֵירְכָ֥א סוֹף-פָּסֽוּק

מֵירְכָ֥א טִפְחָ֖א סוֹף-פָּסֽוּק

טִפְחָ֖א סוֹף-פָּסֽוּק

Zakef section

Zakef divides Etnahta and Sof Pasuk into smaller ideas, but only if they already have a Tipha. Revi'a, Pashta and Yetiv suubdivide Zakef into even simpler ideas. Zakef-Katon (a.k.a Katon) is more common than Zakef-Gadol.

Common Patterns

זָקֵף קָטֹן

זָקֵף קָטֹן אֶתְנַחְתָּא

זָקֵף אַזְלָא גֵּרֵשׁ פַּשְׁטָא זָקֵף קָטֹן

זָקֵף קָטֹן

זָקֵף קָטֹן רְבִיעַ
(see Yetiv card)

זָקֵף קָטֹן רְבִיעַ
(see Yetiv card)

Tevir section

When a Tipha idea has three or more words, it needs to be subdivided. We use Tevir for this subdivision.

Common Patterns

טִפְחָא תְּבִיר דַּרְגָּא

טַרְחָא תְּבִיר מֵרְכָא

טִפְחָא תְּבִיר אַזְלָא

טִפְחָא תְּבִיר מֵרְכָא

טַרְחָא אֶתְנַחְתָּא

TORAH TROP

זָקֵף־גָּדוֹל

Common Patterns

זָקֵף־גָּדוֹל

Zakef divides Etnahta and Sof Pasuk into smaller ideas, but only if they already have a Tipha. Revi'a, Pashta and Yetiv subdivide Zakef into even simpler ideas. Zakef-Gadol is only found on short words and it never uses a Link.

סֶגוֹל

Common Patterns

זָקֵף אֶתְנַ֑ח
סֶגוֹל רְבִ֑יעַ
סֶגוֹל טִפְּחָ֑א אֶתְנַ֑ח
סֶגוֹל פַּשְׁטָ֑א

סֶגוֹל

Segol divides Etnahta into smaller ideas, but only if it already has a Tipha and at least one Zakef. Revi'a, Pashta, Yetiv, and Zarka subdivide Segol into simpler ideas. Segol never appears on the first word of a verse.

TORAH TROP

Common Patterns

רְבִיעַ

When Tipha, Zakef, or Segol need to be subdivided and they have one or two Tevirs, Revi'a is used as the Divider.

תְּבִיר

If a Tevir, Pashta, Revi'a or Zarka needs to be subdivided, the subdivider is usually Geresh or Gershayim.

Common Patterns

פַּשְׁטָא

יְתִיב פַּשְׁטָא

יְתִיב מֻנַּח פַּשְׁטָא

אֶצְטָא פַּשְׁטָא (rare)

פַּשְׁטָא

Pashta is only used on the last or second-last syllable of a word. If a Pashta is needed on the first syllable, we use Yetiv, instead. Yetiv never uses a Link.

Common Patterns

תְּבִיר

מֵרְכָא תְּבִיר

תְּבִיר

If a Tevir, Pashta, Revi'a or Zarka needs to be subdivided, the subdivider is usually Geresh or Gershayim.

TORAH TROP

Common Patterns — מַהְפָּךְ פָּזֵר

אַזְלָא גֵּרֵשׁ

פָּזֵר

Pazer is used to subdivide Tevir, Reviʿa, Pashta, and Zarka. Pazer can be linked to up to six Munahs.

Common Patterns — תְּלִישָׁה־גְדוֹלָה

אַזְלָא גֵּרֵשׁ

תְּלִישָׁה־גְדוֹלָה

When Tevir, Reviʿa, Pashta, or Zarka need to be subdivided, Telishah-Gedolah is sometimes used. When the accent is not on the first syllable, a second Telishah-Gedolah is often added to mark the stress. Telishah-Gedolah can be linked to up to six Munahs.

27

TA'AMEI HA-MIKRA: TROP CHARTS
HAFTARAH TROP

Let's face it: learning trop can be very difficult. Most of us are used to the idea that each musical sign represents a single tone, but with trop, most signs (*ta'amim*) represent musical phrases. To add to the difficulty, there are 28 separate trop signs — each with a unique musical phrase, and sometimes the phrasing changes depending on the combination of *ta'amim* (though very few readings contain all 28 *ta'amim*). Sure, you can find sheet music to help you out, but if you're like me and don't read music, you might wind up more confused. Oy!

I developed the charts in this section to help people like me. Most of the *ta'amim* are grouped into sequences that are used commonly in the Tanah. The grids enable the teacher and the student to chart the music as it goes higher or lower.

These charts have proven quite helpful with my own students. I hope you find them just as useful!

אֶתְנַחְתָּא

Etnahta divides a verse into two broad ideas. Tipha, Zakef, Segol, and Shalshelet then divide Etnahta into smaller ideas. Etnahta always comes after Tiphah.

Common Patterns
מֵירְכָא טִפְחָא מוּנַח אֶתְנַחְתָּא
טִפְחָא מוּנַח אֶתְנַחְתָּא
מֵירְכָא טִפְחָא אֶתְנַחְתָּא
טִפְחָא אֶתְנַחְתָּא
מוּנַח מוּנַח אֶתְנַחְתָּא

What's the point of all this trop?

Apart from musical notations, the trop (or, more properly, *te'amim*) tell us where to put the correct emphasis in each word and sentence. They also function as grammatical and syntactical notations, telling us when to pause in our reading, when to read quickly, etc. So we don't just read the punctuation — we sing it! There are seven distinct vocal systems for chanting the Tanah. Most people are familiar with Torah and Haftarah. See if you can find out what the other five are!

Haftarah Trop

Sof-Pasuk — סוֹף־פָּסֽוּק

Sof Pasuk is also called סִלּֽוּק (Siluk). It marks the end of a verse. Tipha and Zakef subdivide Sof Pasuk into smaller ideas. Sof Pasuk always comes after Tiphah.

Common Patterns

מֵרְכָ֥א טִפְחָ֖א סוֹף־פָּסֽוּק

מֵרְכָ֥א טִפְחָ֖א סוֹף־פָּסֽוּק

טִפְחָ֖א סוֹף־פָּסֽוּק

מֵרְכָ֥א טִפְחָ֖א סוֹף־פָּסֽוּק

מֵרְכָ֥א טִפְחָ֖א סוֹף־פָּסֽוּק

מֵרְכָ֥א סוֹף־פָּסֽוּק

טִפְחָ֖א סוֹף־פָּסֽוּק

Etnahta — אֶתְנַחְתָּ֑א

Etnahta divides a verse into two broad ideas. Tipha, Zakef, Segol, and Shalshelet then divide Etnahta into smaller ideas. Etnahta always comes after Tiphah.

Common Patterns

מֵרְכָ֥א טִפְחָ֖א אֶתְנַחְתָּ֑א

טִפְחָ֖א אֶתְנַחְתָּ֑א

מֵרְכָ֥א טִפְחָ֖א אֶתְנַחְתָּ֑א

אֶתְנַחְתָּ֑א

מֵרְכָ֥א אֶתְנַחְתָּ֑א

HAFTARAH TROP

Common Patterns

זָקֵף־קָטֹן

Zakef divides Etnahta and Sof Pasuk into smaller ideas, but only if they already have a Tipha. Revi'a, Pashta and Yetiv subdivide Zakef into even simpler ideas. Zakef-Katon (a.k.a Katon) is more common than Zakef-Gadol.

Common Patterns

טִפְחָא

When a Tipha idea has three or more words, it needs to be subdivided. We use Tevir for this subdivision.

HAFTARAH TROP

Common Patterns

זָקֵף-גָּדוֹל

זָקֵף-גָּדוֹל

Zakef divides Etnahta and Sof Pasuk into smaller ideas, but only if they already have a Tipha. Revi'a, Pashta and Yetiv suubdivide Zakef into even simpler ideas. Zakef-Gadol is only found on short words and it never uses a Link.

Common Patterns

זָקֵף אֶלֶֹ

חֶרֶב וּמָגֵן וּמִלְחָמָה

סֶגוֹל מַחֲנֶה

סֶגוֹל מַחֲנֶה

סֶגוֹל

Segol divides Etnahta into smaller ideas, but only if it already has a Tipha and at least one Zakef, Revi'a, Pashta, Yetiv, and Zarka subdivide Segol into simpler ideas. Segol never appears on the first word of a verse.

Common Patterns

לְמַֽעַן

מַפְּכָֽא מֵרְכָֽא | מֵרְכָֽא מַפְּכָֽא

מֵרְכָֽא מַפְּכָֽא מַפְּכָֽא

רְבִיעַ

When Tipḥa, Zakef, or Segol need to be subdivided and they have one or two Tevirs, Revï'a is used as the Divider.

Common Patterns

מֵרְכָֽא מַפְּכָֽא

מֵרְכָֽא אַזְלָֽא

מֵרְכָֽא אַזְלָֽא
(a.k.a. אַזְלָֽא וְגֵֽרֶשׁ)

מֵרְכָֽא אַזְלָֽא מַפְּכָֽא
מַפְּכָֽא אַזְלָֽא־גֵּֽרֶשׁ

מֵרְכָֽא מַפְּכָֽא

גֶּֽרֶשׁ

If a Tevir, Pashta, Revï'a or Zarka needs to be subdivided, the subdivider is usually Geresh or Gershayim.

Common Patterns

פַּשְׁטָא

מֻנַּח פַּשְׁטָא

מַהְפַּךְ פַּשְׁטָא מֻנַּח זָקֵף

פַּשְׁטָא מֻנַּח זָקֵף

מֻנַּח פַּשְׁטָא מֻנַּח זָקֵף

(rare)

פַּשְׁטָא

Pashta is only used on the last or second-last syllable of a word. If a Pashta is needed on the first syllable, we use Yetiv, instead. Yetiv never uses a Link.

Common Patterns

גֵּרְשַׁיִם

מֻנַּח גֵּרְשַׁיִם

גֵּרְשַׁיִם

If a Tevir, Pashta, Revi'a or Zarka needs to be subdivided, the subdivider is usually Geresh or Gershayim.

HAFTARAH TROP

Common Patterns

פָּזֵר

פָּזֵר

Pazer is used to subdivide Tevir, Revi'a, Pashta, and Zarka. Pazer can be linked to up to six Munahs.

Common Patterns

מְהֻפַּ֡ךְ־לְגַרְמֵ֤הּ

מְהֻפַּ֡ךְ־לְגַרְמֵ֤הּ

When Tevir, Revi'a, Pashta, or Zarka need to be subdivided Telishah-Gedolah is sometimes used. When the accent is not on the first syllable, a second Telishah-Gedolah is often added to mark the stress. Telishah-Gedolah can be linked to up to six Munahs.

34

INCREDIBLY HANDY TIME LINE

The dates here are approximate. The two main columns compare the Tanah's chronology with samples of writings from ancient Yisra'el's neighbors that relate to events in the Tanah. There are also thousands of Hebrew inscriptions and documents dug up by archeologists, but unfortunately I don't have space to mention them all! The narrow column on the left shows you when the books of the Torah and *Nevi'im* (Prophets) <u>take place</u>, **not** <u>when they were written</u>. See if you can locate your own Torah / *Haftarah* readings on this time line!

WHEN TORAH BOOKS TAKE PLACE	TIME LINE FROM THE TANAH (TORAH & PROPHETS ONLY)		STUFF WRITTEN ABOUT YISRA'EL BY YISRA'EL'S NEIGHBORS
BERESHIT	First Jewish family: Avraham, Sarah, Yitzhak, Rivkah, Ya'akov, Le'ah, Rahel, Yosef and all his brothers	**1600 BCE** 3600 years ago	
		1500 BCE 3500 years ago	
		1400 BCE 3400 years ago	
	Benay Yisra'el in Mitzra'im	**1300 BCE** 3300 years ago	
SHEMOT, VAYIKRA, BAMIDBAR, DEVARIM	Time of Moshe and the Exodus	**1200 BCE** 3200 years ago	Egyptian Pharaoh Merneptah records a list of nations living in Cana'an. "Yisra'el" is included in the list (1205 BCE)
	Benay Yisra'el capture land of Yisra'el		

When *Navi* Books Take Place	Navi Books	Events	Timeline	Historical Records
YEHOSHU'A, SHOFTIM		Benay Yisra'el in Mitzra'im Time of Moshe and the Exodus Benay Yisra'el capture the land of Yisra'el and settle it. Time of the *Shoftim* (tribal chiefs).	**1200 BCE** 3200 years ago **1100 BCE** 3100 years ago	Egyptian Pharaoh Mernepta<u>h</u> records a list of nations living in Cana'an. "Yisra'el" is included in the list (1205 BCE)
SHEMU'EL		Time of King Sha'ul, King David and King Shlomo; First Temple is built; Kingdom of Yisra'el established	**1000 BCE** 3000 years ago	
1 MELA<u>H</u>IM		Kingdom splits into Yehudah and Yisra'el (922 BCE) Book of *1 Mela<u>h</u>im* describes invasion of Yehudah by Pharaoh Shishak	**900 BCE** 2900 years ago	Egyptian Pharaoh Shishak writes a victory monument about invading the region in and around Yisra'el
2 MELA<u>H</u>IM AMOS, HOSHE'A, NA<u>H</u>UM, MICAH, YISH'AYAH #1		Time of Eliyahu and Elisha; Book of *2 Mela<u>h</u>im* describes a rebellion against Yisra'el by Mesha, king of Mo'ab; *2 Mela<u>h</u>im* also describes war between Aram, Yehudah, and Yisra'el	**800 BCE** 2800 years ago	King Mesha of Mo'ab makes a stone monument describing his rebellion against Israel; Anonymous king of Aram makes a stone monument describing war with Yehudah & Yisra'el
		Ashur conquers Yisra'el (722-720 BCE) Books of *2 Mela<u>h</u>im* and *Yish'ayah* describe Assyrian invasions of Yehudah and Yisra'el	**700 BCE** 2700 years ago	Assyrian kings Tiglath-Pileser III and Shalmaneser V write inscriptions and wall carvings about conquering Israel; Assyrian king Sennacherib writes inscription about his invasion of Yehudah
2 MELA<u>H</u>IM TZEFANYAH, YIRMIYAH, YE<u>H</u>EZK'EL, YISH'AYAH #2, OVADYAH		**Bavel conquers Yehudah (590's-586 BCE)** Yerushalayim destroyed (586 BCE)	**600 BCE** 2600 years ago	**Babylonians write inscriptions about their invasion and conquest of Yehudah**
HAGAI, ZE<u>H</u>ARYAH, HABAKUK, MAL'A<u>H</u>I		Cyrus of Persia allows exiles to return from Bavel; Temple rebuilt; time of Ne<u>h</u>emiyah & Ezra	**500 BCE** 2500 years ago	Persia conquers Babylon; Persian King Cyrus II writes inscription about his policy of allowing all exiled people to return home

HAGAI,
ZEHARYAH,
HABAKUK,
MAL'AHI

Cyrus of Persia allows exiles to return from Bavel; Temple rebuilt; time of Nehemiyah & Ezra

Persia conquers Babylon; Persian King Cyrus II writes inscription about his policy of allowing all exiled people to return home

500 BCE
2500 years ago

400 BCE
2400 years ago

Books of the Torah, Prophets, and other pieces of literature are edited and compiled into the Tanah

300 BCE
2300 years ago

Greek Empire defeats Persia and takes control of the land of Israel

Jews successfully rebel against Greek Seleucid Empire & establish kingdom of Judea (Hanukah)

200 BCE
2200 years ago

100 BCE
2100 years ago

Time of the Mishnah

(final compilation roughly 200 CE)

Dead Sea Scrolls are written and hidden in caves in the Judean Desert

Roman Empire takes control of Judea

1 BCE / 1 CE
2000 years ago

Jews rebel against Rome; Jerusalem and the Temple are destroyed (70 CE)

Romans build a massive arch with carvings that depict the victory over the Jews

200 CE
1800 years ago

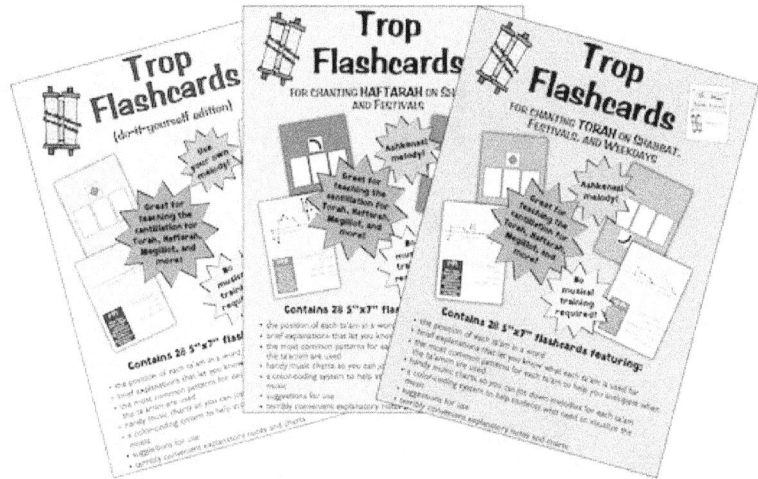

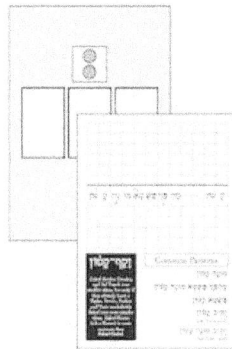

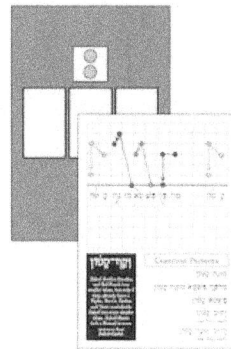

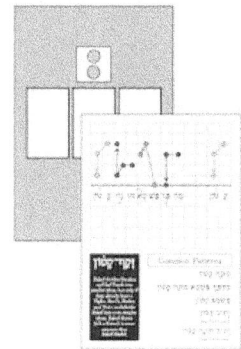

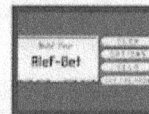

HEBREW
Punch-Out Letters

IDEAL FOR...
Bulletin Boards ✿ Class Projects ✿ Displays & Announcements ✿ And much more!

✱ Long-lasting, durable card stock!

✱ Bright colors!

✱ Reu...

Actual Size & Type

Each set contains...

Also includes vowels, punctuation, and Torah trop!

Suggestions? Questions? Want to say 'hi'?
Visit us at
www.adventurejudaismessentials.com

© Adventure Judaism Classroom Solutions, Inc.
Made in Canada.

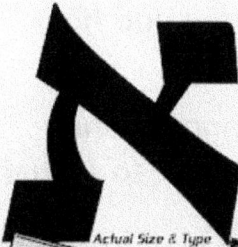

RED!
YELLOW!
BLUE!
WHITE!
PURPLE!
ORANGE!
GREEN!
BLACK!

Available in 8 stunning colors in varnished card stock that won't fade!

Each set includes enough letters, numbers, punctuation, vowels, and trop to make full sentences!

Punch them out and pin them up! Great for...

✓ Displays & Announcements

✓ Manipulatives for Special Education

✓ Bulletin Boards

✓ Class Projects

✓ Bar/Bat Mitzvah

✓ Much, much more!

אִמָּא, מָצָאתִי
נָ36! אֶפְשָׁר
לְהַחֲזִיק?
(בְּבַקָשָׁה...)

(our imagination)

וּמֹשֶׁה בֶּן-מֵאָה
וְעֶשְׂרִים שָׁנָה בְּמֹתוֹ
לֹא-כָהֲתָה עֵינוֹ
וְלֹא-נָס לֵחֹה:

(Deuteronomy 34:7)

A fun way to learn about the Holy Days and the order of the Hebrew months!

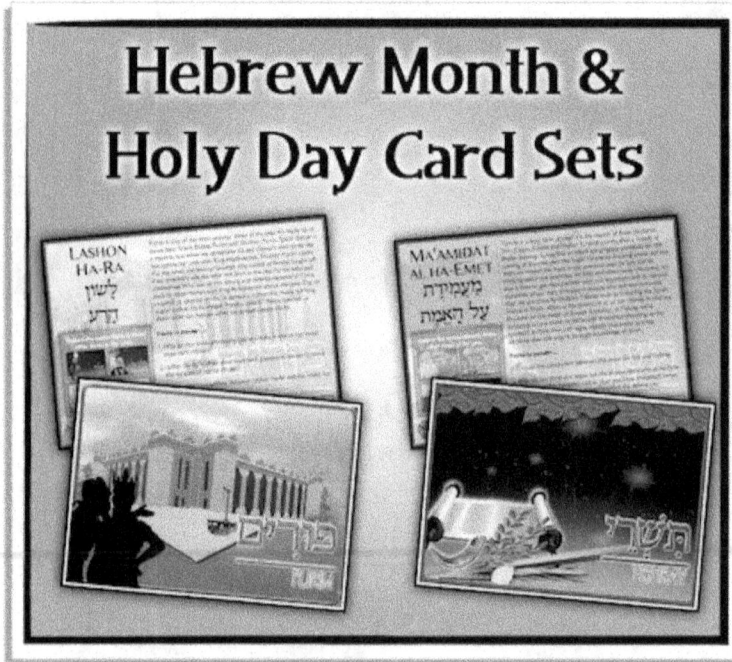

The Hebrew months and Holy Days come alive with the Hagim & Hodashim Cards series. Meet any classroom or programming need with our large display cards, flashcards for small groups, or playing cards for active learning through games. Use them for:

√ **Learning the order of the Hebrew months and Holy Days**

√ **Connecting months and events inthe year to Jewish values**

√ **Designing a values-based program for the year**

√ **And more!**

Hebrew Month & Holy Day Card Sets

The 11"x8" display cards are perfect for word walls, sorting games, class displays, and more.

The 7"x5" flashcards are great for working with small groups.

The 4"x3" playing cards are great for match games, fish, memory games, and more. Suggestions for games are included.